LYNN ELDRIDGE

BIPOLAR TO BELOVED

A JOURNEY FROM MENTAL ILLNESS TO FREEDOM

THE COMPANION WORKBOOK

ENDORSED BY DR. RANDY CLARK, DR. HEIDI BAKER, DR. RODNEY HOGUE, AND DR. MIKE HUTCHINGS

LYNN ELDRIDGE

BIPOLAR TO BELOVED

A JOURNEY FROM MENTAL ILLNESS TO FREEDOM

©2022 by Lynn Eldridge, Bipolar to Beloved: The Companion Workbook
Editor: Loral Pepoon, Cowriterpro Editorial Services
Published by: Crown Creations, LLC
Cover Design and Interior Design: Lisa Thomson, BZ Studio
Cover Photography: rachelholdenphotography.com

ISBN: 978-1-7374906-2-3

Scripture quotations marked AMPC are taken from the Amplified Bible Copyright 1954, 1958, 1962, 1964, 1965, 1987, 2015 (only use the last year corresponding to the edition quoted) by The Lockman Foundation.

Scripture quotations marked MSG are taken from THE MESSAGE, copyright © 1993, 2002, 2018 by Eugene H. Peterson. Used by permission of NavPress. All rights reserved. Represented by Tyndale House Publishers, Inc.MSG

Scripture quotations marked NABRE are taken from the New American Bible, revised edition © 2010, 1991, 1986, 1970 Confraternity of Christian Doctrine, Inc., Washington, DC All Rights Reserved.

Scripture quotations marked NIV are taken from THE HOLY BIBLE, NEW INTERNATIONAL VERSION®, NIV® Copyright © 1973, 1978, 1984, 2011 by Biblica, Inc.® Used by permission. All rights reserved worldwide.

Scripture quotations marked TPT are from The Passion Translation®. Copyright © 2017, 2018, 2020 by Passion & Fire Ministries, Inc. Used by permission. All rights reserved. ThePassionTranslation.com.

Printed in the United States of America

Special thanks to Edna Riley, a wise mentor, teacher, and a patient friend, who said, "Good for you if you have a testimony of losing 600 pounds but tell me *HOW* you did it."

Edna's words were the catalyst for me to create the workbook companion for my book. Edna also echoes the sentiments I've heard from so many others. And one day, I listened and wrote! This workbook will take you through all the practical steps of how I went from Bipolar to Beloved.

Let's dive in!

CONTENTS

AN OVERVIEW:
WHO I WAS AND
HOW GOD CHANGED ME

I WAS LIED TO.

I was told I was bipolar, I had an anxiety disorder, borderline personality disorder (having no stability with myself or others), eating disorders, and addiction. I was suicidal, and my doctors for more than 35 years told me that this is the way I'd always be, so we just needed to find the 'right' medication combination.

What came first? The chicken or the egg?

What came first: the chemical imbalance or my ways of thinking that created the chemical imbalance?

I didn't know that I could be addicted to negative emotions. It was a cycle. Negative emotions would trigger a dopamine release in my brain. Dopamine is a hormone in your brain that releases after emotional experiences. Subconsciously, I liked that dopamine release, and I would want or need to react negatively again to get another release of dopamine.

I would be dopamine depleted and would have to have a bigger negative emotion to get the release of dopamine. I was addicted to the destructive emotions. I needed more and more extremes of behavior, and both having those negative emotions and the corresponding dopamine release were habit forming.

But here's the bottom line…I had been lied to all my life.

I don't have a chemical imbalance today. I'm not bipolar. I don't suffer from anxiety anymore. I am stable and emotionally well-balanced. I'm not addicted to anything but love, peace, and joy.

What changed? I changed! I am not a victim of my past or what people have said about me. I don't get my acceptance from outside of me. I don't think the way I used to think, and my brain has healed. I want to show you the steps I've taken that have brought me balance.

This is not a religious teaching. I've been in nearly every denomination, religion, New Age, occult, etc. I've lived in India and Thailand thinking those religions might lead me on a better path. Yet, in the end, it was Jesus Christ who saved me. The religious people killed Jesus. I don't want a "religion." I want transformation.

My main concern for all people is that we don't function the way we were created to and then we "short out." My iPhone will only function if I follow the ways it was designed to function. I cannot apply Android instructions for my iPhone and expect it to work. It will leave me frustrated, angry, upset, and unable to understand why it doesn't work.

As I just mentioned, my iPhone only works the way the creator designed it to function. It's not that the maker of the phone is mean or punishing. It's that I don't understand how it's made. I don't know what I don't know. Until I seek out the operating manual—the instructions—I will remain upset at my phone that won't work. My phone isn't "mentally ill." There's nothing "wrong" with it. I'm just using the wrong manual.

The operating manual for our lives is based on love. Hate, much like the wrong instructions, will "short out" our operating systems. And when this "short" happens, it's easy to get angry with God for "letting" it happen. I spent most of my life living by MY ways and wondering why most everything "happened to me." But life didn't put walls in my way, I walked into them. I didn't understand there was only one way I was created to function—no matter what I believed.

At around 17 years old, King David wrote Psalm 119, the longest chapter in the Bible. In this chapter, he says in so many words to God, "I need to know your laws, commandments, precepts, statutes, etc." At just 17, King David knew that the only safe place to be was in the ways of Wisdom. He knew anything else is a trap. Anything else is a lie.

My culture doesn't tell me who I am today. I was not designed by my culture; I was designed by God. The church couldn't save me. The people couldn't save me. Prescription drugs couldn't save me. Jesus Christ saved me! Learning His ways, His Truth, His life, and turning mine over to Him saved me.

Yes, in this world we will have trouble. Yes, we will always face trials. But by turning to His Word and His ways, we become aware of how we may be bringing trouble on ourselves out of ignorance. From there, instead of mimicking the cultures around us, we can start to reflect the image of our King.

Finally, in God's ways, we can find healing and rebirth! We can be restored to our default operation, designed by our Creator. We can apply the tools of our Father's Kingdom to achieve the full potential that He designed for each one of us.

When do we begin to learn the 'tools' of our Father's Kingdom? Now!

Where do we start?

Here!

I'M SO GLAD YOU ARE HERE—WELCOME!

You've opened this workbook because there's something in your life that needs to change. Maybe you're battling an addiction. Maybe you have a mental "disorder" that's running your life. Maybe you continue to make choices that are landing you in unproductive or harmful situations. Or maybe you have no idea why, but you feel that your life is not going in the right direction. Whatever it may be, this workbook was designed to help you identify what those self-destructive ways are, how you can turn it around for yourself, and then how you can plan for and achieve a better future.

The contents of the workbook are the basic steps that I took as I began to learn how to get free of a lot of crippling issues in my life—crippling to the point of suicide. Applying these tools and gaining understanding from this work will be the beginning of a wonderful, perhaps even mind-blowing journey! Let's get started!

I'M SO GLAD YOU ARE HERE— WELCOME!

THE STARTING POINT: WISDOM

The Kingdom of God is built on RIGHTEOUSNESS, PEACE, AND JOY. I looked up the word "righteousness" in a dictionary, and two of the synonyms were right-mindedness and right-wiseness. Wisdom will restore us to our right mind. Jesus Christ is Wisdom. No evil can function in wisdom, and what was happening in my mind, as you'll find in my book, was evil. When I looked up the word "evil," one of the definitions I found was "pain and poverty." That got my attention! For years, I suffered in pain and spiritual poverty, because I was lacking God's wisdom.

I had to learn how to live in God's wisdom because my best thinking had me suicidal. Today, I am in love with the One who is Wisdom, and I want to know all about Him and His ways. I am forever grateful for this process, and it didn't happen overnight for me. Bipolar, depression, suicide, addiction, and eating disorders left me within months of learning and applying what I didn't learn in churches or even in Bible college. Nor did I learn this in any of the occult religions I tried, in pursuit of answers.

I learned to live in God's wisdom by giving the God of Love, Jesus Christ, all I had, which at the time, was nothing but pain and brokenness. Yet, the God of Mercy and Compassion showed up, and He continues to show up as I continue to seek His beauty every day, all day.

One of the first things this workbook will take you through is the keys I took to learn how to live in God's wisdom. Wherever you're coming from, whatever evil you're facing in your life, you can find freedom through God's wisdom, as I have. I pray this is a great beginning for you, as well as for the many who at this point in their lives don't know how to apply the simple, yet profound Gospel of Love. I invite each of you to walk with me as we learn how!

A Note About Your Expectations...

Before we go too much further, I want you to know: I didn't take one math class in first grade and then know everything to know about math. In fact, to this day, I am still sharpening my math skills. It's the same way with learning how we were created by the Creator to live. I continue to learn, apply, grow, repeat. Throughout this beautiful journey, be patient with yourself. Be kind to yourself. He always shows up when we seek Him. God's presence rarely looks like what we think it will look like, but it's always better than we could imagine—if we don't give up.

8

1 KEY 1: WILLINGNESS—What does it look like to be willing?

So, I told the Lord Jesus one day, "I've tried it Your way before, and 'it' didn't work." Actually, I was on a three- or four-day drug and alcohol binge when I remember having that conversation with Him. Why would I even be talking to Him in that state of mind? I believe His heart was broken for me, and He was letting me know He was there and has always been there. Yet, I wasn't willing to stop the behavior, as I didn't know His ways—I just thought I did.

I thought God's ways were about going to church on Sunday, Wednesday, praying sometimes, and reading the Word sometimes. I thought Christianity was a bunch of rules I had to follow, but that I would never be able to live up to. But I didn't know how to be all in. I had only known my family's ways, my church's ways, and the world's ways. None of these ways ever helped me heal my heart or get to the root of my trauma and turmoil (either inflicted by myself or others). I didn't know how to quit participating in my self-destructive ways, even during my time at Bible college. The only option I had was to medicate the pain with something—anything—everything outside of me. Besides, I was having "fun," right?

Do you know the fruit of the pain and trauma? Do you want to not just medicate it, but eradicate the pain of the past so that it no longer destroys you from the inside out? I didn't care that my life was a total train wreck. But when the false gods of money, of food, sex, alcohol, and self-destructive painkillers wouldn't work anymore, I had to change or die. Depression, anxiety, anger, hate, control, etc., had quit distracting me. Suicide was all I could think about.

I became willing. I cried out to God in anger and pain, hating myself and everything about life. I didn't want to kill myself; I just wanted the pain to stop. I was so, so broken that I was desperate enough to do the only thing left to try: surrender. I told Him I'd give Him one more chance! Just show up or kill me. I put a demand on Jesus, saying, "Let's go big or go home. I'll do anything You say one more time. I am all in!" I realized that either I let go of my ways, or I'm going to die.

Please ask yourself, and fill in the blank with either yes or no:

1. Are you willing to quit doing what's not working and go ALL in? _____.
   If not, you won't get much, if any, inward or outward transformation.

2. Are you willing to accept the fact that there are suggestions that you can follow, and that learning a new way will take time, but if you don't quit, miracles will happen? _____

3. Are you willing to tell Jesus Christ that you will give Him all you have one more time? _____

4. Excuses are skins of a reason stretched over a lie. Are you willing to give up all excuses? _____

5. Are you willing to have the "no" taken out of your vocabulary when it comes to learning new skills to recognize and receive help and healing? _____

6. Are you willing to immerse and saturate yourself in Jesus music, Jesus books, Jesus TV/podcasts, Jesus YouTube teachings, surrounding yourself with people who love Jesus? _____

7. Are you willing to quit hanging out with the old friends who have lives that are broken like yours? And are you willing to surround yourself with people who have lives they're excited about living, full of life-building habits and hope? _____

8. Are you willing to learn and apply new keys to bring healing to your heart, even if it feels uncomfortable? _____

9. Are you willing to take 100% responsibility for your feelings and the way your life is? _____

10. Are you willing to take this level of willingness into all areas of your life and keep it up and keep it up and keep it up…? _____

11. Are you willing to learn the difference between facts and truth? What people and experts may say or believe, versus what God says, no matter what the 'facts' look like? _____

If you answered yes to most of these questions, let's go! Let's dive into the rest of the workbook. It's time to do whatever it takes to be all in and have your life be transformed from the inside out! The measure of willingness you put in will be the measure of hope that will fill your heart and mind.

Let's do as the following passage says — let's respond, understand, and receive revelation!

> "If you understand what I'm saying, you need to respond!" Then he said to them, "Be diligent to understand the meaning behind everything you hear, for as you do, more understanding will be given to you. And according to your longing to understand, much more will be added to you. For those who listen with open hearts will receive more revelation. But those who don't listen with open hearts will lose what little they think they have!" (Mark 4:23–25 TPT).

2 KEY 2: FORGIVENESS—What does it look like to live in forgiveness?

I had a "right" to be offended! Many things that happened to me were unjust. I was wronged. Some things were extremely traumatic. People will always give you a "right" to be offended.

Forgiveness doesn't mean that what was done to you was okay; it does mean that we are tied to the offender spiritually *until* we forgive and release that person. Somehow, we think we are punishing the other person when we don't forgive. The truth is, not forgiving punishes and destroys the one holding the offense. We actually build walls up in our heart to keep the pain from happening to us again. But the walls in our heart only keep the pain inside, and we end up getting hurt again and again as we remember what caused the pain.

When we forgive, we release any demand for that person to acknowledge the pain they caused, and we release any demand for punishment. I used to want the offender to feel the same hurt and pain as I did. I wanted them to understand the pain they had caused and pay the consequences for what they did to me. That thinking made sense to me, but that retribution never happened. Usually, they went on with their lives, possibly without a single remembrance of my painful event. They didn't live it over and over in their minds. And as a result, I would be caught up thinking, *What was wrong with THEM? See how they destroyed my life?*

The truth was that I destroyed my own life by holding bitterness against the offender. What doesn't get healed by forgiveness will come out sideways. Unforgiveness opens a door to torment—emotionally, physically, psychologically, or all the above. And when we let torment in, we tend to be drawn to people who are in the same pain, and who justify and blame others for the problems in their lives. We stay in these same cycles of pain, and then we medicate the pain through food, addictions, sex, shopping, etc. until we have extreme consequences in our lives.

But God has provided the answer. The antidote (also known as anti-foolishness) is forgiveness. Forgiveness is the key to freedom in every area of life. If there's no forgiveness, there is no freedom. Forgiveness is power! Getting out of God's way and letting Him bring justice to any and every situation relieves us of the pain that is turned inward, destroying us.

When the clutter of our unforgiveness toward people and places gets cleaned out of our hearts, and we start filling our hearts instead with peace, we can begin to heal. Maybe we need to forgive others, ourselves, and even God, where we think that He has let things happen, has let us down. Most often, we need to learn to forgive ourselves. God wants to fill us with His love as we repent, turn from hate, and learn to receive love.

I remember feeling peace for the first time after I did some forgiveness work. I didn't know if I liked it, as peace was so unfamiliar to me. At the time, I was addicted to drama. Extreme negative emotions release dopamine into the brain, causing a "high." But then you get the consequences of extreme depression.

I don't chase drama anymore. Now, I'm in love with Love. I'm free to love you, God, and myself. Love is intoxicating, and there are no consequences of being loved by the God of love.

1. List at least four people that you need to forgive in one column. In the second column, write why you have resentment against them. With some people, you may have many reasons that you resent them, so list them all.

_____   _____

_____   _____

_____   _____

_____   _____

_____   _____

2. Write a letter to each person, pouring out your heart's pain and emotions. Let them know that you forgive them, and that you're going to release them. There's no need to send the letters. Give the pain and resentment to God. Pray for them to get healing for any of their own hurts, because hurt people hurt people. Then burn the letters. Leave the ashes of pain in the past. Describe how you felt after you wrote and burned the letters.

_____

_____

_____

_____

_____

3. List at least four things you've done for which you need to forgive yourself.

_____

_____

_____

_____

_____

4. Say, "I choose to forgive myself. I decide to no longer hate, judge, or condemn myself." Regret is not a friend. Know that the Lord is a Redeemer, and His promise says He will use all things, ALL things for our good.

5. Acknowledge any anger and unforgiveness you might have toward God.

    God, I forgive you for: _____

_____

_____

_____

_____

6.   Repeat these words: God, will you forgive me for misjudging you, and would you heal my heart?

Regardless of how much you work through forgiveness, the only way to be offended is if you "take" offense. It is a conscious choice whether to be offended or not. The only way to be free and remain free is for you to become unoffendable.

3   KEY 3: ATTITUDES AND EXPECTATIONS: How do our attitudes form our expectations and our outcomes?

Attitudes

Attitudes are contagious! I remember being in grade school and some friends were saying, "I hate math." I wanted to fit in with my friends, so I began to say, "I hate math, too!" The truth is, I didn't hate math, but since my cool friends hated math, I figured hating math was cool, so I probably should hate it too. I didn't realize that this attitude change toward math made my grades change too…and not for the better.

A year or so later, I sat next to twin boys that were so cute. I heard one of them say, "We love math!" I liked the boys, so I said, "I love math, too!" I ended up being in accelerated math and algebra classes for years. Our attitude really does determine our aptitude.

Proverbs 4:16 (AMPC) says negative attitudes blind people. Literally. They cannot see the way out of negative cycles, possibly because they don't realize it's not *normal* to function with an attitude of ingratitude. Complaining is an attitude of unbelief. It blinds us, just like it blinded the Israelites in the wilderness. Instead of an 11-day journey, it took them 40 years, and they all died in the wilderness, except Joshua and Caleb. These two men were the only ones who walked into their destinies and into the promises of God.

Proverbs 4:23 (TPT) says, "So *above all*, guard the affections of your heart, for they affect all that you are. *Pay attention* to the welfare of your innermost being, for from there flows the wellspring (seasons) of life."

I didn't realize that my bad attitude led to negative words, thoughts, and behaviors that were self-sabotaging. A friend of mine shared with me that every time he saw an old friend of his, he could feel the bitterness "buzzing" right underneath his skin, right where his heart was. But we weren't created to house bitterness. God has a good attitude. He is content. He is not stressed out. Jesus is The Prince of Peace. He does not have an anxious, fearful attitude. We were not created to be stressed, anxious, or fearful. And when we let these attitudes win, we open the door to self-destruction.

Expectations

I did not realize that my negative attitudes created an expectation that the same negative experiences in my life would happen again. For example, my family had a financial trauma, and as a kid I was afraid of being broke and hungry. This fear was generational, as my grandparents and parents really struggled through the Great Depression. There was great poverty and hunger when my parents were growing up. They worked very hard and eventually had an amazingly successful business. Yet, no matter how much money they had, there was such an attitude of fear and an *expectation* of poverty and pain. Their past struggles seemed to linger in the present. A fearful attitude and negative expectations are like an app running in the background of our minds, draining our hearts' batteries of the joy, peace, and prosperity of our present and future.

There was *never enough*. My attitude was, *I am not good enough. God is letting me down.* And my attitude created the expectation that maybe I wasn't good enough. My expectations formed through the mirror of my heart, which was how I saw most people and situations in my life—but my perception was sometimes imagined. When I thought God was letting me down, I was really seeing the illusion that I was conditioned to see through my generational attitude.

Good news! We can recognize our negative attitudes and fear-based expectations and learn about God's plans for us—to give us a hope and a prosperous future.

Jeremiah 29:11 (NIV) says, "For I know the plans I have for you," declares the Lord, "plans to prosper you and not to harm you, plans to give you hope and a future."

He is the God of love. The enemy is the god of fear.

I was living from fear, always *expecting* the other shoe to drop.

Today, I expect goodness and mercy to follow me all the days of my life. That's what God says in His Word. So, I listen to God's Word, and I ask Him to remove my attitude of fear and to show me how to be. As a result, I have expectations of goodness and experiences that are life-building.

1. What is the attitude of your heart when you think of your family? Your finances, your job, your weight, etc.?

_____

_____

_____

_____

2. What negative attitudes from childhood did you pick up and now believe to be *normal*?

_____

_____

_____

_____

3. What do you think God's attitude is towards you? Do you think that He is angry or disappointed?

_____

_____

_____

_____

4. What is your attitude towards yourself? Is it critical? Regretful? Hard and harsh?

_____

_____

_____

_____

5. Do you have ungodly attitudes and unforgiveness? If so, please describe what these attitudes are and who you hold unforgiveness toward.

_____

_____

_____

_____

6. Are the attitudes you have written down fear-based? Or are they love-based? How do you think you can change them?

_____

_____

_____

_____

7. Do some of the attitudes you have come from past hurts or traumas? If so, describe your hurts and the resulting attitudes.

_____

_____

_____

_____

_____

8. Do your attitudes reveal judgments (a judgment is actually a harmful observation tied to a negative emotion) from those past hurts? Are your attitudes now projecting onto God, yourself, and others, creating an *EXPECTATION* that the same type of hurts will always happen to you?

_____

_____

_____

_____

Make a list of 10 things you are grateful for.

_____

_____

_____

_____

_____

_____

_____

_____

_____

9. Make a list of times when God and others have blessed you during the last 10 years.

_____

_____

_____

_____

_____

_____

_____

_____

10. Change your focus from what your past says to what God says. What do you think he is saying about you today?

_____

Notice the two halves of the verse below. Recognize the first half as coming from ungodly attitudes...bitter attitudes, angry attitudes, critical attitudes, etc., while the second half comes from Godly attitudes of the heart.

> Let all bitterness and indignation and wrath (passion, rage, bad temper) and resentment (anger, animosity) and quarreling (brawling, clamor, contention) and slander (evil-speaking, abusive or blasphemous language) be banished from you, with all malice (spite, ill will, or baseness of any kind).

And become useful and helpful and kind to one another, tenderhearted (compassionate, understanding, loving-hearted), forgiving one another [readily and freely], as God in Christ forgave you. (Ephesians 4:31–32, AMPC).

Say out loud daily, "I expect great love and good to come my way today! I have an attitude of gratitude! I am getting more and more breakthrough and joy as I *put* my hope and expectations in my loving King Jesus Christ! He only does good, which destroys evil (pain and poverty). I choose to agree with Him for the plans for my life. Today is a good day to have a good day!

4 KEY 4: BOUNDARIES—
Where is your circle of peace?

Boundaries protect us. They keep the guards on our heart, as Proverbs 4:23 reminds us. The ocean and the land have boundaries. If the waters overflow onto the land, it has the potential to destroy everything inhabiting the land. The countries of the world have boundaries. Conflicts happen when one country invades or crosses another country's border—another term for boundary. Likewise, crossing boundaries created by the law are problematic, as is crossing boundaries in relationships with others and with God.

God's Boundaries

God tells us all about His nature and character. He gives us laws, precepts, commandments, statutes, and His ways—not because He's religious, but because they are the protective ways of a good, loving Father. Religion is punishing. God corrects and disciplines us, but it is to train us in the ways we are created by Him to live our best lives. He says repeatedly in His Word: IF you follow my ways… THEN you will be blessed. But IF NOT, there will be a curse (a consequence). He has given us choices, also known as free will.

God does not curse us if we defy the laws of gravity because we don't believe in gravity or if we don't know about the physics of gravity. It doesn't matter what we believe. It doesn't matter if we know about gravity or not. Gravity exists, and you cannot break the law of physics —instead, they will break you. Hosea 4:6a says, "My people are destroyed for lack of knowledge." And all we have to do to get that knowledge is to listen to God. What God says is Truth. He is the Way, the Truth, the Life (John 14:6).

If we try to swim with our mobile phones, they might short-circuit and die. But it is not the creator of that phone that is "punishing" us or "letting this happen." We need to know the way the phone's creator made it to function. If as a child, we had punishing caregivers, we might believe God to be hard and punishing, as the most influential caregiver. Therefore, we tend to think that God is angry at us. But this concept of His anger is not in agreement with His Word, His nature, or His character. Knowing the difference between the truth of Scripture and what our feelings might perceive is why it is so important to spend time with our Loving King in His presence, in worship, and in His Word.

1. Define what you think God is like. (Ex: angry, disappointed, perfectionistic…)

    _____

2. Define the God you want. (Ex: kind, happy, loving…)

    _____

3. Consider your perception of God. Do you recognize His nature from His Word, or is your view of God influenced by a critical parent or a preacher who taught that God was angry and disappointed in people?

    _____

Boundaries With Myself

I have to enforce boundaries with myself. Today, because I believe that God is Love, I have been able to receive His Love, learn His ways and love myself. I thought there was *something wrong with me*. Others told me there was something wrong with me. That's not what God says. He says that I'm created in His image, and there is nothing wrong with Him. I just believed the lies from others even from childhood and lived unknowingly from those false beliefs.

But today, I am responsible for my own life and my own choices. I have chosen to learn God's ways, and He continues to heal and restore my life. I used to be a victim, and since I didn't know God's ways, I was unaware that I was volunteering to be more victimized. When I hated myself, I had no value for myself, and I chose people to be in my life who also didn't value themselves, so why would they value me? Choosing people who don't know God leads to more hurt, trauma, and self-destruction.

I also had to learn functional boundaries. I have to choose to take care of my health by making healthy food choices. I work out. I have to learn the discipline of showing up to work, going to bed on time, managing my money, seeking God and His will for my life. I had to choose my new friends wisely, and I had to develop consistency and stability in my emotions. I had to grow up.

Today, I believe in God who is always good, who loves me. He defines me. I was created to be loved and to love. I respond by learning how to please the One my soul loves, and in turn, I've learned what it looks like to love myself.

Answer the following questions for yourself:

1. Where can I learn more skills, and how can I be more responsible?

    _____

    _____

    _____

    _____

    _____

2. What aspects of my life lack discipline or self-control?

    _____

    _____

    _____

    _____

    _____

3. Do I do what I say I am going to do? If not, why not?

    _____

    _____

    _____

    _____

    _____

4. Do I tend to make a lot of excuses or blame others for my troubles? Why or why not?

_____

_____

_____

_____

_____

5. Where and from whom can I learn how to grow, mature, and respond in healthy ways to everyday life responsibilities? List two to five possibilities.

_____

_____

_____

_____

_____

Boundaries With Others

But I *love them.*

They need me.

I have to take care of them.

If I say "no," it will hurt their feelings.

There is a law of sowing and reaping that God put into place. If we *sow* foolishness, we will *reap* the consequences. My parents reaped the consequences of my destructive lifestyle by bailing me out of situation after situation, calling it *"love."* By doing so, they practiced co-dependence with me, and they ended up reaping my consequences for me—to both my detriment and their own detriment. They were actually enabling and supporting my self-destruction, and I brought all that trauma into their lives.

They only knew the boundaries that they had experienced in their families, and they didn't know that love does not mean providing a safe place for your family member to kill themselves or hurt others. They thought all their actions were to sincerely help me, but they were sincerely wrong. I could have "hit bottom" decades earlier, but I was having *fun* (living irresponsibly), and they were taking responsibility for my consequences.

God intended sowing and reaping as a disciplinary and corrective measure—not an angry and punishing measure. My family used punishment and not corrective discipline because that's how they were raised, and how my grandparents raised them. They weren't bad people. They just didn't know God's corrective ways or boundaries.

Answer the following questions for yourself:

1. In what aspects of my life do I need to learn to say no ? Do I need to say no to friends or to having too many obligations? If you answer yes to these questions, make a list of what conversations you need to have.

   _____

   _____

   _____

   _____

   _____

2. Do I feel false responsibility for the bad decisions of others, especially adult family members? If so, what do I need to change my actions?

   _____

   _____

   _____

_____

_____

3. Am I in situations during which my emotions get out of control because I keep wanting to "help" people who ask for my help but really don't want it? If so, what could I do to change these situations?

_____

_____

_____

_____

4. Am I being a people pleaser or am I being controlled by another? What action would be better for me to take in this situation?

_____

_____

_____

_____

For a more in-depth look at boundaries, I highly recommend the book, _Boundaries_ by Dr. Henry Cloud and Dr. John Townsend.

5	KEY 5: MATURITY—The beauty of balance and maturity, from applying God's wisdom

"The only life worth living is a well-balanced life."
—Jim Rohn, author and motivational speaker

I used to enjoy the extreme highs. Sadly, I believe I was even addicted to the extreme lows. These lows gave me a desperation to find any impulsive "fix" to bring me the false joy and false happiness I was craving. I didn't want responsibilities or disciplines because they would get in the way of my immature impulsiveness, reactions, and cheap thrills. Basically, I was emotionally charged like a three-year-old who is crying one second and the next second distracted by something like a cheap toy or even a bug.

As long as I could, I wanted to *remain, continue, and dwell* in my self-centered, self-willed, self-destructive ways because I was wounded in my heart and soul. I had no conception of the keys that would bring me healing and hope for true joy, true success, and happiness—virtues that we all long for. But learning those keys requires growing up in every area of life. Otherwise, there are consequences, because we were never created to function with false love, joy, or peace.

The "I'll Be Happy When" Syndrome

"I'll be happy when I find the *right person to share life with*." I called it love, but really it was codependency and lust. I'd attach to various two-legged "saviors" who were false loves that failed again and again. But Jesus Christ is TRUE LOVE. He is faithful and has never failed me. He will never leave me or forsake me.

"I'll be happy when I am free to eat, drink and do whatever I want." I called it freedom! I was never satisfied. It turned into an eating disorder that was anorexia, bulimia, and obesity. All of those false comforts brought consequences of addiction, pain, and disease. It was hell.

I had a big hole in my heart that only God can fill.

"I'll be happy when I have the right job and enough money." I called it success. I thought money could buy me love, peace, and joy. There was never enough money to buy off the pain, torment, and suicidal thoughts. I learned the "deceitfulness" of riches. I had a lot of wealth and was trying to not kill myself every day because

I was so miserable. Mark's Gospel tells us that "the worries of this life, the deceitfulness of wealth and the desires for other things come in and choke the word, making it unfruitful." (Mark 4:19 NIV). Even though I'd been in church off and on, God's Word wasn't penetrating my heart because I was deceived with riches and overcome with other desires.

"I'll be happy when something outside of me fixes the issues on the inside of me." I called it peace. The medication of the day in the form of a drug or another substance had the consequences of addiction and side effects. My body built up tolerance and craved more and more until it was controlling me, and I was dependent on it.

The ways of God have taught me how to be balanced and stable. I mature as I apply and discipline myself by responding (being responsible) to His truth about Who He is (His nature and His ways), myself (I was created to be love and act like true Love), you and my life. Let's take a closer look at His truth about how we were created to act in one of the most famous passages in the Bible.

> "Jesus began to teach them:
>
> "What happiness comes to you when you feel your spiritual poverty (*desperation*)! For yours is the realm of heaven's kingdom.
>
> "What delight comes to you when you wait upon the Lord! For you will find what you long for.
>
> "What blessing comes to you when gentleness lives in you! For you will inherit the earth.
>
> "How enriched you are when you crave righteousness! For you will be satisfied.
>
> "How blessed you are when you demonstrate tender mercy! For tender mercy will be demonstrated to you.
>
> "What bliss you experience when your heart is pure! For then your eyes will open to see more and more of God.
>
> "How joyful you are when you make peace! For then, you will be recognized as a true child of God" (Matthew 5:2–9 TPT)

The following are divine exchanges: Beauty for Ashes, Joy for Mourning, Life for Death, Wisdom for Foolishness, His ways instead of my ways because His ways bring TRUE happiness. I am not constantly waiting to be happy when…I have found my joy, and He has a name…Jesus Christ. I asked the Lord to take my pain and brokenness and burn it up until my heart only yearned and burned for more of Him.

Today, I have true happiness. In my past, I made idols of things outside of me. Jesus has filled those places, and yet, there's always more healing. I live in gratitude that I'm not as broken inside as I used to be. He's brought me soooo far.

I still pursue Him, and I receive more and more of His goodness and healing by applying His word and *remaining* in His ways. Instead of remaining in selfishness and the words of the flesh that scream, "I want! I think! I feel!" I get to learn to remain in Him, dwell on Him, follow Him, and continue to abide in His love.

1.   What do you believe will make you happy "when…"?

_____

_____

_____

_____

_____

2.   Would you be *willing* to learn AND apply the Godly disciplines of worship, spending time with the Lord in His presence, seeking Him first daily in all you do?

_____

_____

_____

_____

_____

3. Would you be *willing* to apply *forgiveness* to everyone for everything and anyone for anything on a *continuing* basis?

_____

_____

_____

_____

4. Would you be *willing* to pay attention to your innermost being to do a heart check with your internal/external *attitudes & expectations* on a daily basis, learning to have gratitude as all things work to form our Godly character?

_____

_____

_____

_____

5. Would you be *willing* to study and apply *boundaries* with yourself and others?

_____

_____

_____

_____

6. Would you be *willing* to exchange beauty for ashes by incorporating the responses of Galatians that will bring *balance, maturity* and *stability* to your life?

_____

_____

_____

_____

_____

For help replacing beauty for ashes, as well as replacing selfishness with maturity, let's take a look at what Scripture has to say about these topics.

BEAUTY: "But the fruit produced by the Holy Spirit within you is divine love in all its varied expressions: joy that overflows, peace that subdues, patience that endures, kindness in action, a life full of virtue, faith that prevails, gentleness of heart, and strength of spirit. Never set the law above these qualities, for they are meant to be limitless" (Galatians 5:22–23, TPT).

ASHES: "The behavior of the self-life is obvious: Sexual immorality, lustful thoughts, pornography, chasing after things instead of God, manipulating others, hatred of those who get in your way, senseless arguments, resentment when others are favored, temper tantrums, angry quarrels, only thinking of yourself, being in love with your own opinions, being envious of the blessings of others, murder, uncontrolled addictions, wild parties, and all other similar behavior. Haven't I already warned you that those who use their 'freedom' for these things will not inherit the kingdom realm of God!" (Galatians 5:19–21 TPT, capitalization added for emphasis).

"When your **SELF-life** craves the things that offend the Holy Spirit, you *hinder* him from living free within you! And the Holy Spirit's intense cravings *hinder* your **SELF-life** from dominating you! So then, the *two incompatible and conflicting forces within you* are your self-life of the flesh and the new creation life of the Spirit" (Galatians 5:17 TPT, bold font and capitalization added for emphasis).

VICTORY OVER SELFISHNESS: "Tolerate the weaknesses of those in the family of faith, *forgiving* one another in the same way you have been graciously *forgiven* by Jesus Christ. If you find fault with someone, release this same gift of *forgiveness* to them" (Colossians 3:13 TPT).

"For love is supreme and must flow through each of these virtues. Love becomes the mark of true **MATURITY**" (Colossians 3:14 TPT, capitalization added for emphasis).

"And then our **IMMATURITY** will end! And we will not be easily shaken by trouble, nor led astray by novel teachings or by the false doctrines of deceivers who teach clever lies. But instead, we will remain strong and always sincere in our love as we express the truth. All our direction and ministries will flow from Christ and lead us deeper into him, the anointed Head of his body, the church" (Ephesians 4:14–15 TPT, capitalization added for emphasis).

6 KEY 6: THOUGHTS, MEDITATIONS

The Key to Mental Health:

> As a man thinks, so is he.
> —Proverbs 23:7

> Oh, the joys of those who do not follow the advice of the wicked, or stand around with sinners, or join in with mockers. But they delight in the law of the Lord, meditating on it day and night. They are like trees planted along the riverbank, bearing fruit each season. Their leaves never wither, and they prosper in all they do (Psalms 1:1–3 NLT).

Thoughts in the brain, called neurons, look like "trees." (Dr. Caroline Leaf, *Switch on Your Brain: The Key to Peak Happiness, Thinking, and Health*, Baker Books, 2013.) When we think of repeated thoughts such as, "I am unwanted, I'm not good enough," etc., the negative thoughts actually destroy the "branches" and "leaves" of the neuron, causing them to be unhealthy, dead, and produce no "fruit." So, what we meditate on will bring us life or death.

If you know how to worry, you know how to meditate. If you've ever been offended and thought about the situation later, repeatedly, you know how to meditate. I used to meditate on the painful words, situations, and traumas in my life. Even the pain from childhood where, real or imagined, I felt rejected, neglected, and even mistreated. And whether it's real or imagined, childhood trauma is very real in our minds. My meditation on past traumas stirred up more emotions like regret, fear, anxiety, self-hate, anger. And I lived the pain of yesterday every day.

Through the keys of willingness, forgiveness, healing attitudes, learning boundaries, and emotional regulation through the maturity processes covered in the Part 1 of this workbook, my brain started changing and healing.

Today, I get to meditate on what God says, not what negative words or comments people have said to me or about me. What brought incredible hope for me was recognizing that there are facts (fruit) and there is Truth (what God says). Many different "experts" told me I was mentally ill, and I was always going to be suffering with emotional or mental pain. But God, He says that I have the mind of Christ.

I am the beloved. I am in His image, and He's not mentally ill. I am the head and not the tail. I am above and not beneath. I will prosper in all I do. So, it was suggested to me to choose who I want to believe—people who put a label on me, or the One who created me.

As I *thought* and *meditated* on what God says about me, I started to believe Him. His Word filled me with hope. The more I *meditated* on what the Word says about how He loves me, and the more I came to believe it, I received joy.

Worship is meditation. That's why God wants us to worship Him. The more we recognize Who He is, the more we know who we are. Worship is also filled with gratitude. As our thoughts and attitudes heal, our brains change and become healthy thought trees.

Think on the following thoughts, modified and personalized so that they become your thoughts. In addition to thinking these thoughts, say them out loud to further internalize them.

- I am patient, slow to anger (Proverbs 16:32, modified and personalized).

- I make a clean break with all cutting, backbiting, profane talk. I am gentle with myself and others, sensitive, forgiving just as God in Christ has forgiven me (Ephesians 4:32 MSG, modified and personalized).

- I am a calm and patient woman who knows how to silence strife (Proverbs 15:18 TPT, modified and personalized).

- I love discipline and I love myself (Proverbs 15:32, modified and personalized).

1. What do you find yourself meditating/thinking about while you're washing dishes, driving, getting dressed in the morning? Do those thoughts come from love or hate? Joy or fear?

----

2. Are your negative thoughts about someone or something leading you to forgiveness, even for yourself? Why or why not?

_____

_____

_____

_____

_____

A Bible reading plan can lead you to scriptures to meditate on. Use the emotions you want to overcome as keywords in your search. I recommend the YouVersion Bible app at https://www.bible.com/. I recommend the following plan: *Time For A Turnaround by Lynn Eldridge, Intl.* Will you commit to using this plan or one you find? If you want to search for your own plan, what topic will you search for?

_____

_____

3. What TV, music, movies do you entertain yourself with (meditate on)?

_____

_____

_____

_____

4. What TV, music, movies, books could you eliminate that might reinforce what negativity you want to eradicate from your life?

_____

_____

_____

_____

_____

5. What TV, music, movies, books could you add that could bring you hope?

_____

_____

_____

_____

If you don't know, search on whatever player you have for Christian Contemporary Music. PureFlix is a movie subscription service, and to search for books, look for Christian Inspirational on Amazon.

6. Make a list of emotions or stressful situations that are causing you discomfort and intentionally find meditations that interrupt and oppose the destructive thoughts.

_____

_____

_____

_____

7. What you "feed" will grow. Do you feed yourself (meditate on) love or fear? Explain your answer.

_____

_____

_____

_____

_____

7 KEY 7: WORDS AND DECLARATIONS

"Watch your **words** and be careful what you say, and you'll be surprised by how few troubles you'll have" (Proverbs 21:23 TPT).

I used to talk negatively about myself and others. I didn't realize that these words originated generations before me; I got it from my mother who got it from my grandmother, who probably learned it from the one who raised her (my grandmother was an orphan). But I also didn't realize my negative talk was from bitterness and unforgiveness as well.

As I mention in *Bipolar to Beloved*, I went to a friend's house when I was in grade school, and her mother called me *precious*. Precious was a word that was not spoken over me by my mother. I was shocked. I craved more encouraging words like that, so I was at my friend's house as much as possible so that I could be around her mother. It was so powerful to my little girl's heart. I only remember critical words from my mother. I internalized those critical words and made them my own negative affirmations. I was critical, judgmental, and condemning to myself. I don't think I was aware that there was another way to perceive myself.

You've probably heard the phrase, "You're going to eat those words!" This expression is more than just a saying. And, the words we speak affect both ourselves and others. They fall right into your heart and bring either joy or sadness. But the words we speak also fall into the hearts of others—in fact, they can poison the way others see you and the one you're talking about. For example, if I start telling my friends that our friend Sally isn't trustworthy, soon all of my friends will start to see Sally the same way.

On the other hand, loving words come across as encouraging and honoring. These honoring statements can also change the way others perceive you and the one you are talking about. Just as easily as my negative words can make my friends distrust Sally, my honoring words can make my friends see Sally as God sees her.

I heard a story once about a teacher who held up two red apples. They were both beautiful to look at. Then she firmly pounded one of them on her desk repeatedly. It didn't break the skin so with the eye both the apples still looked beautiful on the outside. Then she cut them in half. The one that had been pounded on was bruised and discolored on the inside. Negative, critical, shaming words might not be visible on the outside, but they always do damage on the inside. The other was healthy and juicy on the inside. Words do matter. Be careful whose words you receive.

We tend to *echo* what we learn from our families and friends. I had to learn to choose my words wisely, because I reaped the negativity I was repeating with my words. Our words have power. The power of life and death is in the tongue. Negative words have the power to affect genes that regulate physical as well as emotional stress. So, it's important to watch the words we listen to and the words we speak, because our words can impact our mental and physical health. No wonder my life improved dramatically as I started reading, hearing, and speaking the words that I was loved by God.

The power of words is like the law of sowing and reaping. If I *sow* kind words, eventually I will also *reap* kindness. And if I am patient and kind to myself, then I can be patient and kind to others. Words will direct your life. Choose to speak positive, life affirming words over yourself and others, and you'll see just how impactful it can be.

The voice we believe the most in life is our own. I used to say negative statements like, "I have the worst luck!" and "There is obviously something wrong with me." By speaking these words, I was actually declaring and affirming a pattern of a downward spiral. I was trained by negative influences in my life growing up, and hearing these negative words repetitively declared around me and they became my declaration too. I internalized these declarations until they became my external reality as well. Today, I know how to change that narrative. I recite, declare, and affirm life-building, motivating, hope-filled and inspiring statements about myself and my life.

Affirmation means to confirm and strengthen. Affirmations can be positive or negative. They will have a positive or negative outcome. Decide, define, and declare your future. Don't let the voices from your past or from others dictate your future.

As we remind ourselves of who we are and how things are going to be, we will be more inclined follow our words up with actions.

1. Speak these words/declarations/affirmations out loud about yourself every morning upon awakening for at least 30 days.

    I, (write your name here) _____ am loving and kind.

    I, _____ am teachable.

    I, _____ am unoffendable.

    I, _____ have life affirming attitudes.

    I, _____ have healthy boundaries with others and myself.

    I, _____ am grateful. This is going to be a great day!

    I, _____ am learning new skills and building healthier neuropathways.

    I, _____ am creative and creating a beautiful life as I focus on beauty.

2. Speak words/declarations/affirmations out loud about the people in your life. Change your focus from cursing to blessing. Declare the good of the people that possibly brought you the most pain by changing your focus.

    I appreciate _____ for the gift of _____ _____ she/he brought into my life.

    I am grateful to my mother for the gift of _____ she brought into my life.

    I am thankful to _____ for the _____ they brought into my life.

When I am dealing with a problem that is causing me some anxiety or emotional pain, I ask God for scripture, as His Word is the prescription for life. Not only do I meditate on them daily, but I personalize them to the first person, and add my name to DECLARE them out loud.

DECLARATION:

I, _____, keep my thoughts (and words) continually fixed on all that is authentic and real, honorable and admirable, beautiful and respectful, pure and holy, merciful and kind.

Try your own declaration based on your favorite life-building scripture. Repeat it daily with the affirmations above and notice how God's Word starts to work wonders in your life.

_____

_____

_____

_____

_____

8 KEY 8: HABITS & BEHAVIORS

Cigarettes can be habit-forming and damaging to your health. So can any negative habit. I didn't realize that I was addicted to self-hate. I had negative habits of complacency instead of life-building habits of willingness to learn and grow. I was in the habit of being offended. You've heard of habitual liars. I was addicted to negativity in my thoughts, words, attitudes, expectations, reactions, and all these painful addictions grew and created more failure and depression.

It was "just the way I am." Or maybe, it was the way I was because I didn't know I had choices. I didn't know it wasn't *normal*, because it was normal for me and the people that I chose to be around. We were all habitual victims addicted to excuses and pity parties. We had to medicate with whatever distraction was available. I was addicted to the drug, alcohol, food, etc. And all of these habits had consequences.

Suicidal pain brought me a "pattern interrupt." Pain is for purpose. If I am on a spending spree (retail therapy), I can be addicted to the excitement or the sale of the day. It does release dopamine. It does make me feel good for a little bit. But then, I need another fix. As I build up tolerance, I need a bigger "hit" of excitement until I am left with a dopamine depletion and the consequences of my behavior.

The good news is there's an antidote to negative habits. To heal ourselves of the self-destruction from negative habits, we can change to healthy, positive, life building habits. Today, I am in the habit of prayer and meditating daily. I wouldn't think of missing a day without journaling. I am in the habit of exercising daily. I hate to miss it. I'm addicted in a very positive way today.

There is, however, a healthy balance — people can get addicted to exercising. There is a road called Wisdom. On either side of that road is a ditch. If you veer too far to the left or to the right of the road, you could end up in the ditch. For example, food is important. Healthy choices are the road of wisdom. Anorexia is a ditch on one side of that road, and obesity is the ditch on the other side of the road. Both ditches cause pain and self-destruction.

Any distortion of an instinct can lead to self-destructive behavior. For example, sex addiction, spending addictions, workout addictions, sugar addiction, etc. I learned that I had emotional addictions. I was addicted to hate. As I learned balance and emotional regulation by feeding myself wise teachings from people who had success in that area, I began to heal. Today, I am in the healthy habit of being grateful, appreciative, and thankful, on a daily basis.

In order to make positive, life affirming changes and not be overwhelmed, therefore procrastinating or overdoing it to the point of pain (like in an exercise routine), we can just change a little bit every day or every week.

If junk food is a problem, then decide to choose one day to find a healthy replacement and remove the temptation from your grocery list instead of deciding to go on a 500-calorie restricted diet for the rest of your life. What one thing can I decide to change this week in my health, finances, etc.? What one life skill could I learn about this week? Examples include: Watch an intermittent fasting video. Watch or read about how to build wealth. Ask myself: What friend do I need to spend less time with, and who has success in an area of my life that I am weaker in who I could ask for help?

What if little changes bring big results?

What if I started looking for mentors that would inspire me and give me hope and advice to make incremental changes?

When I wanted to be free from addiction, I quit hanging out in bars with old friends with the same habits that were killing me. I found people who knew the keys to freedom and asked for help. My life changed one day at a time, and it still does. Change is not comfortable, but comfortability is death to destiny.

1.   Make a list of negative habits and positive habits in your life.

Emotional Habits (Examples)

Anger.	Peaceful
Frustration.	Contentment
Jealousy.	Grateful
Worry.	Calm

_____

_____

_____

_____

_____

2. What are the consequences of not eliminating the negative habits in your relationship with yourself and others?

_____

_____

_____

_____

_____

3. What negative and positive spiritual habits do you have or not have? What 1% change could you make in that area?

_____

_____

_____

_____

_____

4. What negative and positive health habits do you have? What 1% change could you make for the better in nutrition and exercise?

_____

_____

_____

_____

_____

5. What are the possible consequences if you don't make changes?

_____

_____

_____

_____

6. What negative and positive financial and business habits do you have? What 1% change could you make in those areas to improve your life?

_____

_____

_____

_____

7. What are the consequences if you don't do something different?

_____

_____

_____

_____

8. What resources can you find to help you develop skills, habits and value in every aspect of your life?

_____

_____

_____

_____

_____

9 KEY 9: JUDGMENTS/PERCEPTIONS: Reflections through attitudes

"If you judge people, you have no time to love them."
—Mother Theresa

I'd been told about judgmental people. You're not supposed to judge, right? But what is a judgment? There is good judgment, which is for your protection, right? How do you know how you're supposed to use judgment? I read somewhere that eliminating judgment from your life is a powerful life changer. I had no understanding of the power of eliminating judgment until one day a woman cleared that up for me. A judgment (harmful) is actually an observation tied to a negative emotion.

For example:

My friend Janie and I met for lunch about four times a week for about eight years. Janie was usually late. No problem. I sat in the car and sent emails while I waited for her to tell me she'd arrived. It didn't bother me or hurt our friendship.

But when my mother was late...that was a different story! I had a very negative emotion tied to that!! She was selfish and uncaring about my thoughts or feelings. How could she do this again?! Those thoughts created a bitter root judgment, which, like a boomerang, came right back at me in my life.

Have you ever said, "I'll never be like my mother!" Then, what happens? You find yourself using the exact same words, doing the exact same things for which you judged her. Maybe you don't even recognize it in your own life. Maybe you can't see it because the attitude and judgment has blinded you, and you don't understand the cycle that keeps repeating itself throughout generations.

Bitter judgments distort our perceptions. For example, if I judged my mother for being a certain way, then I start to see other women in authority throughout my life in the same way. To make that double trouble, bitter judgments toward parents is also dishonoring to a parent. Any time someone has any issue in their lives, it usually goes back to dishonoring a mother or father.

No kidding. Even if we were extremely young children when we judged our parents, we need to forgive the parents and then ask God to forgive us for judging and dishonoring our parents (and thereby also dishonoring God and ourselves).

Bitter root judgments can be contagious as a person talks about their judgments to others, and these judgments will also distort the perceptions others have about the one being talked about.

There's a story of Edison. I've learned that a teacher of his sent him home one day with a letter to his mother. It said something along the lines of "Your son is addled (mentally ill). We won't let him come to school anymore." However, his mother read the note to little Thomas this way, "This school is too small for him and doesn't have enough good teachers for training him. Please teach him yourself." Several years after his mother's death, he found the folded paper in old family things. As he read it, he cried and wrote in his diary: "Thomas Alva Edison was an addled child that, by a hero mother, became the genius of the century." (English book Georgia.com)

What people say to you or about you will change your perception, but it doesn't mean it's true.

Do you think that maybe many of us have been living from another person's negative judgment about ourselves? Possibly a parent in anger said something to you that has changed your perception of yourself to this day. Did a friendship or a past relationship not end well and things were said to you that were negative judgments that you possibly internalized and believe?

One day, I asked a 75-year-old woman if I could help her with some work that she was doing on a computer that she was obviously struggling with. She replied to me, "No, you're too stupid to help." At that time, my heart broke for HER because now I know that's how she was talked to and it's how she feels about herself. Her perception was distorted about herself and others because of a negative judgment. She's lived her whole life believing the lie that she's stupid. Today I know that hurt people hurt people. We are all hurt somewhere. No one has "arrived" at perfection and no one will, in this life.

We are all responsible for giving and receiving a hurt.

1. Forgiveness is key. Recognize where past hurts are infiltrating your current perceptions. Forgive that person and yourself for receiving the lie. Who in your past do you need to forgive?

    _____

    _____

_____

_____

_____

2. What are the lies from these hurts and what does God's loving truth say about you?

_____

_____

_____

_____

_____

3. Who do you need to ask to forgive you for making harsh judgments against them?

_____

_____

_____

_____

_____

4. Identify and write out attitudes and declarations you can adopt to replace the lies to change your perception of yourself and others.

_____

_____

_____

_____

5. Look for repeated patterns where you "felt" (rejection, like a victim, not good enough, etc.) and ask God where that lie began. Look for childhood perceptions that seem to continue throughout your life and forgive, releasing them and yourself from them as you also forgive yourself.

_____

_____

_____

_____

6. Under what circumstances have you made negative judgments against the most influential parent or authority from your childhood? Ask God to forgive you and also forgive yourself. Recognize the situations you may be living in your current life in the same manner as the one you judged negatively. Describe these circumstances and situations.

_____

_____

_____

_____

7. Ask Jesus Christ to come and heal your heart from this hurt and pain. Give Him the negative emotions. Ask Him what He says about this situation.

_____

_____

_____

_____

_____

DECLARE:

I don't judge, criticize, condemn and I'm not judged, criticized, or condemned. I choose to love and be loved.

Above all else, guard your heart (mind), for everything you do flows from it (Proverbs 4:23 NIV).

10 KEY 10: VISION/GOALS

"Twenty years from now you will be more disappointed by the things you didn't do than by the ones you did do. So throw off the bowlines. Sail away from the safe harbor. Catch the trade winds in your sails. Explore. Dream. Discover." [2] —H. Jackson Brown Jr., *P.S. I Love You*

Martin Luther said, "There are two days that matter. This day and that day." By "that day," he was referring to the day we face God accounting for our lives.

John Bevere said, "We will not be judged according to our sins...But we will be judged for how we responded to God and His Word in this life—and rewarded accordingly." [3]

Proverbs talks about drifters and the wayward. They're going nowhere, doing not much of anything. Is that what being busy means? Are we glorifying being "busy," this buzzword of the day, above being destined?

Having no goals or intentions for your life used to be considered as a vice. Drifters seemed to be glorified in movies, to the point where now it's part of our culture. No wonder there's no satisfaction or contentment in the world and everyone chases the addiction of the day. I understand completely. "Without a vision, the people lose restraint" (Proverbs 29:18, NABRE).

What do you want in your life? What did you dream of as a kid, teen, or young adult? What generational gifts do your parents have? What kind of jobs do you gravitate toward? God will use everything good and not so great for your good.

I challenge you to sit down with a pen and paper. Write 1 to 10 on the lines at the end of this section and ask God what is written on your DNA and why you were put here on earth. I challenge you to wait and be still. See what comes to you. If nothing today, try again and again. My dreams were buried under 52 years of trauma, pain, and self-destruction. I just got intentional one day after my mentor sat me down and talked to me.

She said, "My biggest concern for you is that you'll end up at the end of your life and realize you have blown past your destiny." Little by little, after I got intentional and asked my Creator what the vision was for my life, I began to remember some things, and then some more things. Now, I see more clearly where my dreams and passions collide. Yet, it was all because of the love of God and my love for Him.

It's a love story. What is written on the pages of your heart's desires? If it benefits yourself and others as well, you are probably on the right track.

Or you can end up at the end of your life and realize it's too late to fulfill your dreams. How you knew that *someday* I can write the book. Or *I'll get around to it when*... We tend to think we have all the time in the world. I have two family members who died before the age of 19 years old. We have no idea what tomorrow will bring. Today is a present. Grasp it and get intentional IF you want your best life for yourself and your family.

1. What 10 dreams of your heart can you identify?

2. Set small goals in all areas of your life (family, health/nutrition, spiritual and emotional growth, education, finance/job, etc.

_____

_____

_____

_____

_____

_____

3. What have you been saying that someday when (fill in with an excuse here) I'll start the class, run the 5K, save for the house, get my degree, etc?

_____

_____

_____

_____

_____

4. What can you put on a do Not do list? (Time wasters)

_____

_____

_____

_____

5. What one goal if you achieved it this year could change everything in your life?

_____

_____

6. Who are the people you need to take a break from?

     _____

     _____

     _____

     _____

     _____

7. Where are you going to be in five years? You will be somewhere! What goals
    do you have?

     _____

     _____

     _____

     _____

     _____

8. What skills/education do you need to develop that would bring value to your
    life and the lives of others?

     _____

     _____

     _____

     _____

9. Who can you find mentorship through to help you? It may be through books, YouTube, courses, a local group (like a writer's group, neighborhood 5K group, etc.)

_____

_____

_____

_____

_____

10. Who could you possibly get to be an accountability partner? 85% of people reach their goals if they have an accountability partner. Only 15% reach their goals if they do not have accountability.

_____

_____

Check out goal setting advice by Brian Tracy. He's written about 90 books on goal setting. He's also on YouTube.

> Now may God, the fountain of hope, fill you to overflowing with uncontainable joy and perfect peace as you trust in him. And may the power of the Holy Spirit continually surround your life with his super-abundance until you radiate with hope! (Romans 15:13 TPT).

CONNECT WITH ME!

If you are ready to start putting the pieces of your life back together with God by learning how to train your thoughts, attitudes, and behaviors, I have resources available for you on my website: lynneldridge.com. Check it out to learn the ways in which God leads me and others through the healing process.

I also mentor people, and I am a Restoring the Foundations minister. To learn more about Restoring the Foundations, visit

restoringthefoundationsinternational.org.

I am available for speaking, leading seminars, and more. My passion is helping people to find freedom and to become well-balanced in all areas of their lives. Speaking topics include breaking cycles of self-sabotage, power to change, wisdom, and more.

I'd love to connect with you! Find me at:

www.lynneldridge.com
www.instagram.com/lynneldridgeofficial
www.facebook.com/lynneldridge.us

NOTES

1. *Goodreads*, "Quotable Quotes," accessed September 22, 2022, https://www.goodreads.com/quotes/2887-if-you-judge-people-you-have-no-time-to-love.

2. *Goodreads*, P.S. I Love You Quotes, accessed September 22, 2022, https://www.goodreads.com/work/quotes/41658-p-s-i-love-you-when-mom-wrote-she-always-saved-the-best-for-last.

3. *Facebook*, John Bevere, accessed September 22, 2022, https://m.facebook.com/JohnBevere.page/photos/as-believers-we-will-not-be-judged-according-to-our-sins-jesus-paid-the-price-to/10157414062068011/.